Villainous Weapons of Persuasion

By Ben Settle
©2019

Ben Settle

Villainous Weapons of Persuasion

*"You either die a hero or you
live long enough to see yourself
become the villain."*

~ Harvey Dent, aka "Two Face"
The Dark Knight

Copyright ©2019 by Settle, LLC and MakeRight Publishing, Inc.

All rights reserved.

ISBN: 978-1088755952

Villainous Weapons of Persuasion
Table of Contents

Legal Notices Even Villains Dare Not Ignore!	**7**
Who is Rood?	**9**
Introduction - The Villain's Armory of Persuasion	**11**
1 - How to Seize Control of Minds You Wish to Persuade	**17**
2 - The "N-Word" That Makes Ordinary Men Quake in Terror	**28**
3 - The Paradox of Persuasive Imperfection	**37**
4 - Making the Skeleton Dance	**45**
5 - How to Give People No Choice but to Believe You	**54**
6 - The Spear of Influence That Impales All Resistance to Doing as You Say	**63**
7 - How to Slash Away Skepticism	**71**
8 - The Shameless Secret of Having Celebrity-Like Preeminence	**78**
9 - The Fastest Way to Get Unquestioned Compliance from People Ever Invented	**84**
10 - How to "Defang" the Snakes of Slander, Smears, and Personal Attacks	**89**
Dastardly Disclosures & Disclaimers	**97**

Ben Settle

Villainous Weapons of Persuasion

Legal Notices Even Villains Dare Not Ignore!

This book is Copyright © 2019-2020 Ben Settle (the "Author"). All Rights Reserved. Published in the United States of America. The legal notices, disclosures, and disclaimers in the front and back of this book are Copyright © 2009-2011 Law Office of Michael E. Young PLLC, and licensed for use by the Author. All rights reserved.

No part of this book may be reproduced or transmitted in any form or by any means, electronic or mechanical, including photocopying, recording, or by an information storage and retrieval system — except by a reviewer who may quote brief passages in a review to be printed in a magazine, newspaper, blog, or website — without permission in writing from the Author. For information, please contact the Author by e-mail at www.BenSettle.com/contact or by mail at that same URL.

For more information, please read the "Disclosures and Disclaimers" section at the end of this book.

First Edition, August, 2019

Published by Settle, LLC (the "Publisher").

Villainous Weapons of Persuasion

Who is Rood?

Rood is an entrepreneur, author, and self-described "Anti-professional." He is also a master of influence and persuasion and spends all his time in his Lair writing books, newsletters, and twisted monster novels to finance his world domination plans.

The authorities are aware of Rood's Villainous ambitions. And it amuses him how they can do nothing to stop him, because he masterfully uses a "loophole" in the law that says it's not illegal to plan to take over the world, since no crime has (yet) been committed.

Rood makes no attempt to hide his real identity, his business dealings, or his Mission to force the world to submit to his will. Through his books about persuasion and Villainy, he openly mocks his hero enemies. And the planet's leaders, military, and police are terrified of the coming day when he decides to make his move...

Villainous Weapons of Persuasion

Introduction

-

The Villain's Armory of Persuasion

"The cunning warrior attacks neither body nor mind...we attack his heart!"

— The Green Goblin
Spiderman

Welcome to this final volume of my Villains of Influence trilogy.

The first book *Persuasion Secrets of the World's Most Charismatic & Influential Villains* was the "ground floor" field manual showing exactly what attributes make men attractive, persuasive, respected, influential, wealthy, and admired by other men and loved by dames. It was the figurative donning of your Villainous Garb of Charisma: The dark cloak, the silver skull-handled cane, the gold signet ring, the concealed bullet-proof Kevlar vest, the villainous sunglasses, etc.

The sequel, *Super Villains of Persuasion*, was then the figurative construction of your hidden chateau's Lair of Influence — strategically placed at the top of a treacherous mountain, complete with a moat, a stocked fine wine cellar, a full staff of henchmen to do your bidding, and all the weapons and instruments of conquest you require.

And now it's time to arm your Lair with said weapons of conquest with this final volume:

"Villainous Weapons of Persuasion"

While the first two books were focused primarily on the strategies and positioning of creating persuasion, charisma, influence, and confidence… this last book is your Villainous armory, stockpiled with the weaponized secrets of persuasion and influence that have been polished, sharpened, and loaded by the principles laid out in the first two volumes. When armed to the teeth with the following Villainous Weapons of Persuasion, you can quickly and cleanly

Villainous Weapons of Persuasion eviscerate the arch adversaries of all your influential pursuits, including:

- **Direct competition** — such as other businesses competing for the same customers you wish to sell to, suitors competing for the same dames you desire, or buyers competing for the same possession and property you wish to purchase

- **Skepticism** — that would delay or utterly destroy a person's decision to do as you command

- **Cynicism** — caused by prior bad experiences you had nothing to do with, projection of someone's feelings onto you, or a jaded marketplace

- **Distrust** — in you, your industry, or by the mere fact you are trying to get something from someone (money, time, romance, a favor, their vote, or anything else)

- **Lack of reputation** — from being unknown, new to an area/industry, or simply not having any kind of recognized brand, name, or experience

- **Indifference** — which is the death of all persuasion, and an enemy you must constantly be ready to mercilessly attack at all times

These are the main adversaries that lurk in the hearts of those you wish to persuade and influence. Lesser men never bother to learn about them, much less study how to defeat them. But, when armed with the *Villainous Weapons of Persuasion* inside this book, you can wipe them out with the proverbial snap of your fingers…

As Easily as The Cosmic Villain Thanos Wiped Out Half the Universe!

That's power you cannot buy, steal, or borrow.

It can only be gained and mastered by constant study, practice, and application.

Villainous Weapons of Persuasion

With that said, it's now time to turn the page, pick your weapons, and finish the journey towards Villainy you started two books ago…

Ben Settle

aka "Rood"

P.S. I would be remiss not to repeat this warning from the last book:

> "You can learn much from the Villains inside this book without adopting their wicked ways. For just as a surgeon's knife can be used to cut out a tumor and save a life, it can just as easily be used to impale someone through the chest. And that's why it is of utmost importance you use wisdom and ethics when applying what you learn inside this tome. For without those two attributes, you will almost surely suffer the same ill-fated consequences (and rightfully so) as most of the Villains referenced ultimately did."

Ben Settle

P.P.S. Movie and TV show spoilers abound inside.

Villainous Weapons of Persuasion

1

How to Seize Control of Minds You Wish to Persuade

> *"You don't pay, you know what we do? We cut you around the waist, peel your skin, pull it up over your head and tie knot in it. And you don't die from that. You suffocate."*
>
> — Gennady
> *Limitless*

In the hit TV show *LOST* (about a group of people whose plane crashes on a mysterious island), there is a scene where Dr. Jack Shepherd needs to get a locked Halliburton suitcase containing guns and ammo from the Villainous James Sawyer. The only way to get this case is to persuade Sawyer — who purposely antagonizes and causes mischief to the group, and who is intensely curious about the contents inside — to give it up.

So what does Jack do?

Well, it just so happens Jack has been treating Sawyer for a knife wound. And what Jack does is, he shows Sawyer a bottle of pills and says:

> "That's the antibiotic I've been giving you for the knife wound in your arm. You're right in the middle of the treatment cycle now, if I keep giving you the pills you're going to be as right as rain. But I'm going to stop giving you the pills. And for two days you're going to think you're all good, then it's going to start to itch. The day after that the fever's going to come and you're going to start seeing red lines running up and down your arm. A day or two after that you'll beg me to take the case, just to cut off your arm."

Obviously, Sawyer has no real choice but to give Jack the case.

Villainous Weapons of Persuasion

And the reason why is because Jack gave Sawyer…

A *Vision* of What Would Happen If He Didn't Do as He Wanted!

Listen:

Just as having a Mission is the "linchpin" that made everything inside *Persuasion Secrets Of The World's Most Charismatic & Influential Villains* work better, and having Superior Confidence was the core attribute that made everything in *Super Villains of Persuasion* work better, creating Vision in those you wish to persuade will make everything else inside this book work better.

Now, the king of creating Vision was the late Jim Camp.

He was known as "The World's Most-Feared Negotiator." And not only did he negotiate deals north of a billion dollars, and routinely compete against (and defeat) the toughest negotiators on the planet… but his methodology was so effective…

Ben Settle

The FBI Changed Their Terrorist Negotiation Protocols Because of Him!

As did many of the world's most prestigious business schools — including Harvard, NYU, USC, UCLA, University of California, and Columbia.

Anyway, according to Jim, Vision drives decisions to be made.

Prompts wallets to be opened.

And, when done correctly…

Forces Even the Most Tightly Closed Minds to Change.

Such as the closing argument in the movie *A Time To Kill*.

The movie is about a couple white men who rape a 9-year-old black girl. The little girl's father (played by Samuel Jackson) shoots his child's rapists in an open court house. Since he's a black man in a predominately white county, his chances of not getting the death penalty are slim to none, and he hires a young, idealistic

Villainous Weapons of Persuasion

white lawyer (played by Matthew McConaughey) to defend him.

Long story short:

By the very end of the movie, McConaughey's character is losing the case to the Villainous District Attorney Rufus Buckley. His witnesses have all been discredited. Samuel Jackson's character openly admits he knew what he was doing when he killed the rapists (destroying his insanity plea). And the all-white jurors have even agreed privately with each other the father is guilty.

All of which means the lawyer…

Has Nothing Left But His Closing Argument.

A closing argument based 100% on Vision.

What happens is, he walks the jury through the entire crime — from the two men jumping out and grabbing the little girl, dragging her into a nearby field, binding her, and then ripping her clothes off… to them climbing on one at a time, drunkenly raping her, destroying her womb forever, and shattering her innocence… to next using her for target practice throwing full beer cans at her, tearing the flesh off her bones, and then urinating on her… to finally putting a noose around her neck and hanging her, feet and legs kicking in the air, and then, thinking she's dead, throwing her in the back of the truck and pitching her over the edge, 30 feet down to the creek bottom.

Finally, he ends with:

> "Can you see her? Her raped, beaten, broken body, soaked in their urine, soaked in their semen, soaked in her blood — left to die.
>
> Can you see her?
>
> I want you to picture that little girl.
>
> Now imagine she's white."

It's such a persuasive Vision, even the ambitious D.A. is visibly changed by the argument.

Villainous Weapons of Persuasion

And, Samuel Jackson's character is ultimately found not guilty.

Another master at creating Vision is a man who has been ranked as the NRA's #1 concealed carry instructor — Joe Holdmann. His classes are often booked out months in advance, he rarely has to advertise, and he charges way more than other local concealed carry instructors. And one of the things he does better than anyone else is…

He Creates Can't "Un-see" It Vision!

For example:

He shows his classes a picture of a recently released criminal — walking the same streets many of the students and their children live — who broke into a family's house and threatened their young daughter, but was let go due to overcrowded jails. He also hands out a copy of a recent local newspaper story with a mugshot of a deranged-looking local meth addict accused of threatening a child in her own home while high on drugs (making him impervious to pain), and then says:

"Imagine this guy is in *your* house at 2 a.m. Well, guess what? He's walking your street, right now, too…"

Creating Vision like this is how Joe seizes control of the minds of his students, and persuades them to listen and pay close attention to his 6+ hour classes, to begin carrying as soon as their license arrives, and to want to hire him (and only him) for further firearms training.

Here are some more examples:

- **Jesus Christ** — who created the world's biggest religion using Vision to describe the anguish of hellfire to persuade people to avoid sin, spurn the religious establishment, and sell everything they had to follow Him.

Villainous Weapons of Persuasion

- **The great advertising copywriter Gary Bencivenga** — who persuaded clients to hire him by, amongst other things, giving them a Vision of what it would be like when the mail trucks full of bags of checks and orders came to their offices after running his ads (something that would regularly happen for his clients).

- **A loving mother** — who, to make sure her children never do drugs, routinely shows them YouTube videos of addicts telling their stories of despair, desperately prostituting their bodies out for drug money, with no teeth, repulsive to the opposite sex, sleeping in their own piss and feces, and plagued with nightmares, hallucinations, and excruciating withdrawal pain.

- **Hardline Guatemalan political propagandists** — who, in the 1980s to create distrust of Europeans, told villagers the white tourists they saw taking pictures of them and their kids were plotting to capture, kill, dismember, and sell their organs on the black market — which persuaded mobs of otherwise non-violent people to murder and dismember white tourists on sight. (Yes, Vision can just as easily be *misused* to cause misery and pain, which is why ethics and wisdom must always prevail.)

- **Child privacy advocates** — who, to persuade parents to remove pics of their kids from social media, use Vision to show parents how pedophiles in the dark web are scraping their children's images from even supposedly "safe" accounts and distributing them for their sick and evil agendas.

To sum up:

If you want someone to make the decision to do as you wish, give them a Vision. Doing so lets you all but seize

Villainous Weapons of Persuasion

their minds, and persuade them to willingly, quickly, and eagerly comply with what you want them to do.

2

The "N-Word" That Makes Ordinary Men Quake in Terror

"Then I spoke the Deplorable Word. A moment later I was the only living thing beneath the sun."

— Jadis
The Magician's Nephew

One of the great all-time Villains is the psychopathic Benjamin Poindexter from *Daredevil* season 3. During the show, he stalks a woman he met while working at a crisis hotline. But, he isn't stalking her to kill, harm, or rape her. He is stalking her because he thinks she can help him with his violent urges and rage the way his former therapist did. Only problem is, he accidentally tips her off he'd been following her, creeps her out, and she runs away. When he approaches her on the street again, she naturally recoils. But,

Villainous Weapons of Persuasion

despite her being afraid to death of him, they are in a coffee shop, talking, and laughing just minutes later.

How was he able to "convert" her fear into a friendly chat?

The answer is simple, it's because…

He Gave Her Permission to Say No.

Specifically, by saying:

> **"Please, just hear me out. I'm doing this in public so you'll feel safe. I'll stay right here. I'm not coming any closer. Okay. I am so, so sorry about how things ended the other night. I'm sorry for scaring you. I just wanted to explain myself. When we worked together at the suicide hotline, I saw the way you were with other people. Patient, compassionate, and I really need that right now. My life is out of control. I have no family, and I'm about to lose my job. Please. I just want to**

talk. Anywhere you choose. And if you say no, I'll understand and I'll never bother you again."

As Mr. Poindexter proves, No is not a word to fear like ordinary men do.

It's something to *embrace*.

And even though it sounds like a paradox…

**The Single Best Way
To Get a "Yes" from Someone
Is to Try to Get Them
to Tell You "No."**

Doing so takes all the pressure off.

It lets down the guards of those you wish to influence.

And, it demonstrates zero neediness, creates 100% honest communication, and opens the other person's mind to hearing you out and making a decision favorable to you.

The key is to own this principle as a way of life…

Villainous Weapons of Persuasion

And Not Fake It
Or Use It as a Cheap Trick.

To further illustrate this principle, check this out:

One of my customers was dating a flakey, recently-single dame who was giving him mixed signals, and he wondered if she was still hung up on her ex-boyfriend. This made him admittedly needy and he constantly worried if she liked him or not.

My advice?

In addition to getting his neediness under control, I told him to…

Encourage Her to Go *Back* To Her Ex-Boyfriend!

i.e. Try to get her to tell my customer No.

The result was this:

> **She got back to me, we met up and hung out, got lunch, etc. and yea she's talking to the ex and other guys, she's "confused" etc said she didn't know how to**

break the news to me and other BS so she went radio silent.

So I was just like "yeah that's great you should totally pursue that, give him a chance, see what happens," etc. I was anti-needy the whole time, super relaxed, having fun, making fun of her etc.

She's already texting me saying she "can't wait" to get together again, we should grab drinks soon" so we're getting together in a few days.

She totally revealed her cards. I almost want to call this the "intentional friend zone," ha-ha.

By me doing this she revealed all this stuff about her like how she was fucking her business partner, how she had threesomes with just women, how her ex wasn't interested in sex, and so on. All these stories about her.

Villainous Weapons of Persuasion

Of course, I am just sitting there saying hardly anything, laid back and she's suddenly super opening up to me.

Will we have hook up again? Who knows and after hearing all her stories, I'm not nearly as attracted to her as before. Isn't that interesting how that works? She's got a good social circle, so I don't mind being friends.

Thanks man, for everything

As you can see, not only does trying to get someone to tell you No eliminate all your neediness (real and perceived), but it also has the added benefit of…

Exposing the Hidden Intentions, Secrets, and Agendas Of Those You Wish to Persuade!

This applies to business, too.

Most people hide their high prices and dance around their offer's "flaws." But I want people to tell me No. Thus, I go out of my way to tell people a product is expensive, or that I have no refund guarantees, or that it takes a lot of effort, time, and sacrifice to make what I am selling work.

Doing so not only turns people I don't want away, but also...

Attracts the Very Best and Highest Quality Customers!

Including customers who are happy to pay my higher prices. Who are more likely to refer others to me. And, who often look forward to buying from me again.

Back to Mr. Jim Camp:

He said "No" was the safest place to be in a negotiation. And early in his career, he sold expensive water filters door-to-door part time in a neighborhood with terrible water. The company he worked for gave him a script and he failed for two weeks straight. He couldn't even get people to talk to him. Finally, he threw the script away. And after introducing himself, he asked people how their water was treating their hair, and said if they

Villainous Weapons of Persuasion

didn't want softer hair just to tell him No and he'd leave.

And guess what?

Trying to get them to tell him No like that worked so well, he went back to everyone who hadn't made a decision, gave him a maybe, or put him off… and, one by one, told them:

> **"I just wanted to ask you to tell me 'no thanks' if that is your decision. That way I can close the file and move on."**

By saying just those two sentences asking for a No…

He Made More Money Selling Water Filters Part Time Than He Did as an Airline Pilot!

Which brings me back to the rub:

The best way to get a "yes" from someone is to righteously (not as a trick) try to get them to tell you "No."

It puts all someone's cards on the table.

It takes people off of whatever pedestal you may have them on.

And, it puts you in complete control of your emotions, while making other people feel "safe" to talk to you — without all the pressure, manipulation, and begging lesser men resort to.

Villainous Weapons of Persuasion

3

The Paradox of Persuasive Imperfection

"I've always been a disappointment, to others as well as myself."

— Melik
AKA, the villainous Jamal
Sinbad The Sailor

In the movie *Unbreakable*, the Villain Elijah Price (aka Mr. Glass) has a rare disease called osteogenesis. This is a brittle-bone disorder where a mild injury — even a sneeze, in some cases — can cause fractures. And while this condition gave him obvious disadvantages in life, it also gave him an extremely powerful advantage when it came to influence and persuasion.

An advantage many great Villains have.

An advantage that, believe it or not, is also...

Shared by Many Famously Influential Addicts, Politicians, Celebrities, Salesmen, And Even Serial Killers.

Consider this list of people:

- **Oprah Winfrey** — Who saw more popularity and revenue when she was fat than when she was in shape

- **Donald Trump** — Whose ridiculous hair style and orange-toned skin are mocked, laughed at, and made the butt of jokes the world over, yet despite that has become a billionaire real estate mogul, reality TV celebrity, and President of the United States

- **Ronald Reagan** — Who was called "The Great Communicator" despite constantly bumbling, making gaffes, and sometimes even forgetting what he was saying mid-thought

Villainous Weapons of Persuasion

- **Advertising giant Jay Abraham** — Whose infamous ad selling his sky-high priced consulting services trumpeted (in the headline) his irrational and self-described cowardly fear of flying

- **Serial killer Ted Bundy** — Who sometimes would lure his victims by putting on a cast, faking a broken arm

These people — good or bad, virtuous or sinister — all utilized the Villainous Weapon of Persuasion known as:

"Being Un-Okay"

Believe it or not, being a bit flawed and imperfect gives you influence.

It makes you more "human", and therefore more approachable.

And — for better or worse — people are far more comfortable being around those who appear a bit less perfect than themselves than they are those who appear flawless. This is why people tend to open up the Un-Okay. Listen to the Un-Okay. And, be more easily influenced by the Un-Okay. This is the opposite of most people — especially in the age of social media — where everyone wants to show how strong and powerful they are, desperately hiding their flaws & blemishes to keep people from seeing any of their negative attributes.

Not so the cunning Villain.

He does the exact opposite, and...

Shouts His Flaws From the Rooftops!

And, as you will see in the next chapter, will even *brag* about them.

Being Un-Okay can take many forms:

Such as being a little more negative about your own plans than someone you are trying to persuade is of going along with those plans.

Not having a perfect vocabulary.

Villainous Weapons of Persuasion

Having an obvious physical blemish or handicap.

Showing slightly flawed coordination or social skills.

Not being the best dressed person in the room.

Being a little bit awkward in your mannerisms.

Or any other kind of flaw in your appearance, movements, posture, education, or personality. It can even be something trivial and accidental, such as when world-class sales trainer Tom Hopkins talked about a woman at a job interview who was so anxious she dropped her pen and nervously scrambled for it. That flash of humanity helped her land the job when the interviewer picked her pen up and said:

"Relax, you got the job."

There is great power in being human like this.

In not being threatening and menacing.

And, in making yourself a little more approachable and human.

On the other hand, those who appear too perfect, too flawless, and too immaculate are often...

Distrusted on Sight!

Such as the perfectly dressed and groomed salesman.

The perfectly rehearsed and delivered speaker.

Or the perfectly handled and scripted politician.

There was, for example, calculated reasons why popular Presidents such as Ronald Reagan and Bill Clinton would sometimes wear jeans and work shirts at certain appearances, to look more humble... or why Abraham Lincoln used to purposely dangle his feet close to the ground on a small horse, so he looked out of proportion and weird. Those "flaws" gave them more — not less — influence.

Villainous Weapons of Persuasion

On the other hand:

The distrust caused by perfection and flawlessness is a visceral reaction people usually are not even conscious of, much less can explain. But it's always there...

Lurking Beneath the Surface Of Their Minds.

And it's why even truly vile people — who *should* be distrusted and shunned — like the homicidal Stuntman Mike from *Death Proof* (older, sloppy eater, teetotaler, was able to more easily seduce young women into his frightening car)... or the One Ring-addicted Gollum (gangly-looking, hideous, desperate, was able to manipulate Frodo into turning on Sam to isolate and lead him to Shelob's lair)... or the nefarious Jamal in *Sinbad The Sailor* (fat, clumsy, superstitious, a failure at many professions, and completely non-intimidating, manipulated kings for decades to help achieve his objectives)... or the psychopathic Alex in *A Clockwork Orange* (who faked being lost and stranded to gain access to a residence and torment its occupants)... or Robert Daly from *Black Mirror* (quiet, shy, socially awkward, who was able to easily "steal" the DNA of those he wished to control)... used their Un-Okayness to get what they wanted, despite their inherent untrustworthiness and evil intentions.

This is why hiding your flaws is foolish.

Why it will only make you more distrusted.

And, why...

It Will Ultimately Destroy Your Efforts to Persuade and Influence!

In the next chapter I will show you another way to use your imperfections and flaws to make yourself so persuasive people will almost not be able to resist doing as you command...

Villainous Weapons of Persuasion

4

-

Making the Skeleton Dance

"Santiago's death, while tragic, probably saved lives. And my existence, while grotesque and incomprehensible to you, saves lives. You don't want the truth because deep down in places you don't talk about at parties, you want me on that wall. You need me on that wall."

— Colonel Nathan R. Jessup
A Few Good Men

In *Star Wars: Revenge of the Sith*, Supreme Chancellor Palpatine is disfigured and deformed during a fight with Jedi Mace Windu. He goes from looking regal, respectable, and approachable… to becoming scary, grotesque, and completely repulsive. And so, in order to get the Senate to give him more power to launch his sinister agenda, he makes a speech, saying...

> "The attempt on my life has left me scarred and deformed, but I assure you my resolve has never been stronger...In order to ensure our security and continuing stability, the Republic will be reorganized into the first Galactic Empire, for a safe and secure society, which I assure you will last for ten thousand years."

What happened next?

The Senate grants him all the power he requests. And, it does so without question, hesitation, or delay — even *applauding* the decision.

This is what world-class sales trainer and author Barry Maher calls:

"Making the Skeleton Dance"

It is based on George Bernard Shaw's quote:

Villainous Weapons of Persuasion

> "If you can't hide the family skeleton, you might as well make it dance."

What this means is, instead of hiding the flaws, negative attributes, and drawbacks of whatever you are trying to persuade and influence people to do…

You Brag About Them!

Barry calls it "bragging about the negative."

And it grants you a power of influence few will ever experience simply because, just like being Un-Okay or trying to get a No, the vast majority of men are terrified of admitting their plan's flaws, and resort to playing "twister" around the truth, instead.

The result is more skepticism.

Being ignored.

And, often, complete indifference.

This is why many smart Villains not only admit and outright *brag* about their flaws…

They Turn Them into Reasons To Believe Whatever They Are Saying!

Take the great Villain-creator Walt Disney, for instance.

Marketing genius and "millionaire maker" Dan Kennedy once told the story about how Disney used this principle right before opening Disneyland. At that time, Disney was out of money and still trying to raise funds from investors, and the media was on their way over. But his company was so broke, they didn't even have enough money to remove all the ugly weeds growing around the park and plant flowers to make the place look nice.

Disney's solution?

He went to all the weeds and ugly foliage around the property, and made little signs with exotic, Latin names on them, and then stuck them in front of the weeds to make them seem sexy and interesting. Which meant all those ugly weeds went from being an eyesore and liability, to assets that...

Villainous Weapons of Persuasion

Enhanced the Perception of the Park!

Retailer American Giant did the same with their $89 sweatshirt. Not only was it obscenely expensive, but you had to wait 6-months for it to arrive.

Most companies would hide or downplay that fact.

But American Giant did the exact opposite...

And Boasted About It!

They even put the so-called "drawback" right in the headline. They also bragged when talking to the media about how their merchandise is so popular and high quality, people are happy to wait and pay that much.

The old Avis car ads also did this brilliantly.

One of their most profitable advertisements prominently said:

"We're number 2. Therefore, we try harder."

Here are a few more Making The Skeleton Dance examples from Barry Maher:

- "Are our machines more expensive? Absolutely. Are they less reliable? Absolutely. But, we're the leaders in the marketplace. Why do you think that happens in spite of the fact that we're more expensive, in spite of the fact that we're less reliable?"

- "Are my fees expensive? Absolutely. Why do I charge so much? Because I can — because my clients aren't just willing to pay these kinds of rates, they're happy to pay them for the kind of results I generate. I'm thinking of raising them."

- And when telling his customer he makes a commission on the sale and is therefore biased, he says, "I don't want you to forget I'm on commission here. The more you spend the more I make. Now, let me

Villainous Weapons of Persuasion

tell you why you need to be spending more and making me more money."

And then he goes on to tell the benefits, which are...

Automatically More Believable Because He *Trumpeted* the Negative First!

For a more homey instance, think of an online dating ad from a dame who wanted a handsome, successful, and high-value man, but had a lot going against her:

- Over 40

- Not as attractive as the girls in their 20's and early 30's the men she wanted were looking for

- Three kids

So, what did she do to stand out?

She Turned Those Flaws Into Reasons to Date Her.

Here's how:

She combined trying to get the No with Making the Skeleton Dance by (1) saying she might not be a good match for a man wanting kids and (2) admitting that yes, she's over 40, which means she has to try harder to compete with younger and hotter women. It's also why she is more submissive and agreeable, can't be a ball-buster or shrew, and wants her man to lead her. She also knows she can't afford to let her appearance go, either. And so, she works hard to keep herself in shape, knowing younger and prettier competition are always afoot.

She also talked about her kids, saying:

> "I know you probably don't want to be daddy to another man's children. But that's okay, because they are all older, two of them are in college and never home, the other is at his father's half the time. And when they are home, if you want, they will chauffeur us around so we can go

Villainous Weapons of Persuasion

> to restaurants and wine tastings and not have to drive."

As you might guess, she wasn't on the dating sites long before finding the exact kind of man she wanted. And she did it because she didn't ignore, hide, or pretend her flaws didn't exist. She instead turned them into reasons to date her.

Making the Skeleton Dance is an extremely sharp Villainous Weapon of Persuasion.

But it takes guts to wield.

It requires thinking and planning to execute.

And, it means you absolutely must be comfortable with being Un-Okay.

However, if you wield this weapon wisely, you almost won't be able to help but be the most persuasive man in the room.

5

How to Give People No Choice but to Believe You

> *"The price you pay for bringing up either my Chinese or American heritage as a negative is — I collect your fucking head. Just like this fucker here."*
>
> — O-Ren Ishii
> *Kill Bill: Volume 1*

In the smash hit TV show *Breaking Bad*, Walter White (AKA Heisenberg), in order to save his business of cooking and selling meth from being snitched on by ten different men in three different prisons who have ties to him, decides to have them all killed.

But, he doesn't just have them killed over time.

He does it in a way where all ten of them are killed…

Villainous Weapons of Persuasion

In the Same Two-Minute Period!

After that, everyone reacts differently and readily submits to him.

Including his own lawyer, his business partners, and even his wife. He becomes something truly frightening, and people do exactly as he says, without question.

Such is the unbridled power of the Villainous Weapon of Persuasion known as:

"Dramatic Demonstration"

It's an extremely potent weapon used by great Villains like when drug lord Reese Feldman in *Starsky & Hutch* proves his new kind of cocaine ("New Coke") is untraceable by scent or taste works by tossing a bag of it on someone who had just been mauled by a drug-sniffing dog for holding real cocaine seconds earlier, and the dog doesn't react to it… or when Tokyo crime lord O-Ren Ishii in *Kill Bill: Volume 1* cuts off a henchman's head, holds it up, and drops it on the table to demonstrate what would happen if anyone in her gang ever again questioned her heritage... or when Governor Tarkin in *Star Wars: A New Hope* blows up an entire planet with the Death Star to demonstrate what the Empire was willing to do to any system that got out of line.

Another example:

The late, great world class direct marketer Gary Halbert once told a story about when he was in the military. He was in the barracks when a man named James Scarpelli tried to physically and psychologically intimidate him the first time they met.

Gary's response?

He Picked Up His Foot Locker And Threw It As Hard as He Could at the Guy's Face!

Then Gary said:

> "I don't have any doubts about you being able to kick my ass, but you should have no doubts about you

Villainous Weapons of Persuasion

not waking up the next day after you do it."

Then Scarpelli held out his hand, introduced himself again, and ended up not only being the best man at Gary's wedding, but also was Gary's collector when he became a loan shark.

Here is another example:

In the book *Another Man's War* Sam Childers (i.e. "The Machine Gun Preacher" — a former violent drug-dealer who converted to Christianity, and founded a ministry that leads armed missions to save Sudanese children from being tortured, raped, and murdered) describes how he once worked at an orange grove in Florida. The people who owned the grove hired him to be an enforcer and make sure nobody stole anything. They also ended up hiring some Haitian immigrants who threatened to put voodoo spells on people, scaring the other workers.

To put a stop to this nonsense, Sam picked up a snake he saw in the grove.

Then, right in front of the voodoo-casting Haitians…

He Bit The Snake's Head Clean Off!

After that, they immediately stopped causing any more trouble.

(And did not even dare look at Sam.)

But you don't have to be violent or threaten violence to create a Dramatic Demonstration. There are many ways this can peaceably work in your life.

Such as the story behind the Otis elevator. In the 1800s elevators were notorious for failing and plunging people to their deaths. And because of that, cities did not build skyscrapers or anything taller than a few floors. Until one day, a man named Elisha Otis discovered a way to make elevators 100% safe. However, nobody believed his invention would work. That is, until he went to the New York World's Fair in 1854 and demonstrated his invention. As soon as

Villainous Weapons of Persuasion

people saw his Dramatic Demonstration everyone believed his invention worked. Not long after that, skyscrapers and tall buildings started to be built, city skylines and maps started to change, and history was made. All because, as the world's greatest living copywriter Gary Bencivenga (who I first heard this story from) once said:

"Nothing is more persuasive than a dramatic demonstration!"

- **That's why the best advertisements do it** — like the "Do You Make These Mistakes In English?" advertisement, that ran for 40+ years — which is unheard of in the advertising business.

- **Why the best motivational speakers do it** — like Tony Robbins, with his infamous fire walks.

- **Why the best magicians do it —** like Harry Houdini, who used to demonstrate escaping jails and safes at police departments.

- **Why the best authors seeking fame & credibility do it —** like bestselling author Robert G. Allen of *No Money Down* who would take someone off the unemployment line, drop them in a random city with just a few hundred dollars and the clothes on their backs, and make them rich to demonstrate his methodology.

- **Why the best fitness celebrities do it —** like Jack LaLanne, who used to do feats of strength in his old age, such as pulling 13 boats containing 76 people while handcuffed and shackled, and other "impossible" demonstrations of strength.

- **Why the best marketing specialists who make millions of**

Villainous Weapons of Persuasion

dollars per year do it — doing what are called "hot seats" — where they work without a net to solve peoples' business and marketing problems on the spot.

And, the list goes on…

Moral of the story:

Start thinking up ways to create Dramatic Demonstrations to prove your case when trying to influence and persuade. It will open the most closed minds. Create instant and unshakable belief in whatever you claim. And, most important of all, wipe out indifference, skepticism, and apathy.

For as Bruce Wayne wisely observed in *Batman Begins*:

"People need dramatic examples to shake them out of apathy."

So, go forth and use this powerful Villainous Weapon of Persuasion. The result will be more people believing you, buying from you, and listening to you, without question, without objection, and without procrastination.

Villainous Weapons of Persuasion

6

-

The Spear of Influence That Impales All Resistance to Doing as You Say

"I've always been more curious than cautious."

— Samuel Sterns
AKA "The Leader"
The Incredible Hulk

One of the most terrifying Villains ever created is the insidious Pennywise the clown from Stephen King's novel *IT*. And one of the things that makes him so terrifying is how he is able to lure children to places they would normally avoid — including into dark sewers, abandoned houses, and other frightening places they know better than to venture to.

He does it using a variety of methods, such as making a child see (and then chase) a moving balloon.

Or making someone see a dead loved one.

Or having a victim hear a dead friend.

Or by taunting those he wishes to torment into coming to him.

It almost always works, too — even on the intelligent, the rational, and those who "know" better.

And the evil, blood-thirsty clown does it…

By Creating Curiosity!

Of all the Villainous Weapons of Persuasion, Curiosity cuts deepest — penetrating the psychology in a way where you almost cannot fail in your persuasion and influential goals.

Take the late, great marketing legend Gary Halbert again.

Gary was one of the most revered, respected, and recited marketing and advertising minds on the planet. He routinely wrote ads that completely changed the way entire industries

Villainous Weapons of Persuasion

marketed themselves. And one day he was with his protégé (the late, brilliant copywriter Scott Haines) on his houseboat in Bayside Marina in Downtown Miami, and asked him this question:

> **"Do you know the #1 reason why most people buy something from an advertisement?"**

Scott thought about it and replied:

> **"Sure, self-interest."**

Gary's response:

> **"That's not it... the #1 reason most people buy something is because of curiosity. Self-interest is very important, but curiosity trumps it."**

Gary knew what all rich mail order people have long known:

People will buy sometimes enormously expensive products they did not even know existed five minutes earlier because of Curiosity that...

Ben Settle

Creates an "Itch" That Needs to Be Scratched!

And here's a true story that perfectly illustrates it:

Arguably the #1 phone sales trainer who ever lived was Stan Billue. Stan trained more 7-figure per year earning phone salesmen than anyone else, and started his career by selling investments over the phone. One day, he was doing his sales calls and connected with a doctor. As soon as Stan started talking, the doctor started yelling at him, threatened him, and then angrily hung up on him.

So Stan called the doctor back.

> **"Yeah??!!"**
> **"Doc, before you hang up on me again I have just one question!"**
> **"What?"**

As Stan put it when telling that story, "Who had control at that point?" The answer, of course, is Stan did. He then listened to the doctor vent, tried to get the him to say No, and ended up…

Villainous Weapons of Persuasion

Selling $200,000 in Stocks To a Man Who Hated His Guts Just Minutes Earlier!

And before you even ask, this was no fluke.

Shortly after that, Stan started *seeking out angry* and hostile leads like that doctor — including offering to buy all the other sales peoples' angry leads on the floor he worked, which he then proceeded to sell even more investments to.

The big lesson Stan taught with this story was:

"Curiosity overpowers programming."

In this case, the doctor was "programmed" to hang up on Stan. Most people are when being sold to. But, because Stan created an itch that had to be scratched in the doctor's mind using Curiosity, the doctor had to at least hear him out.

Another example:

Over the past several decades, probably billions of dollars have been collectively generated by churches, publishers, authors, and Bible teachers who focus on prophecy, sell books about prophecy, and are involved with conferences, seminars, movies, novels, and TV shows about prophecy.

Why is this topic so popular?

Because as world renown Biblical scholar Michael Heiser says…

"Biblical prophecy is ambiguous by design."

i.e. it has curiosity embedded within.

The Bible is literally *designed* around Curiosity — and has people constantly searching, studying, and trying to figure it out. This gets people coming back over and over and over, spending money on expensive software, concordances, and interlinears to learn its mysteries, and staying endlessly fascinated by it. That ambiguity creates that overpowering Curiosity to keep even people

Villainous Weapons of Persuasion

programmed to be skeptical coming back to study it, debate it, want to "crack" it, and have all the answers to it.

One more example:

In my business using email, everyone is programmed to delete emails on sight. But if you use Curiosity correctly in the subject lines you won't get deleted. If you use Curiosity correctly in the body of an email, you'll get read. And, if you use Curiosity correctly at the end…

People Will Often Be Very Tempted To Click Over and Buy What You're Selling!

That's why I call Curiosity the "Spear of Influence":

It penetrates the mind fast and sinks in deep.

You can use it to get (and keep) the attention of almost anyone for almost anything you want — whether it's to get them to see a movie… go on a date with you… give you their vote… behave if they are misbehaving… spend money, or anything else. It will "overpower" someone's natural reaction to ignore you, hang up on you, or walk away from you.

So if you want someone to hear you out, use Curiosity.

If you want someone to not be able to ignore you, use Curiosity.

And, if you want someone to do something you ask, use Curiosity.

Doing so lets you create an "itch" that just has to be scratched. And the only way to satisfy that itch is to comply with what you want them to do…

Villainous Weapons of Persuasion

7

-

How to Slash Away Skepticism

"Why are you screaming? I haven't even cut you yet."

— Freddy Krueger
A Nightmare On Elm Street

Let's talk about the Villain of which nightmares are (literally) made:

Freddy Krueger.

He was originally a child murderer so evil the neighborhood parents burned him alive. And to extract his revenge, he comes back as a dream demon — wearing gloves with sharp blades on the fingers, invading the dreams of the children of the parents who killed him, and murdering those children in their sleep.

But it's not the finger knives that make him so dreaded.

Nor is it his burnt flesh.

Or even his evil voice and one-liners before killing someone.

No, what makes him so horrifying the kids do everything they can to stay awake is...

Freddy's Relentless And Persistent Contact!

Here's what I mean:

Freddy comes back night after night... invading his victims' dreams, wearing them down, exhausting them... until, finally, they can't stay awake and he traps them in their own dreams, unable to escape. That Relentless and Persistent Contact gives him preeminence in their minds. Before he even so much as shows his claws, they know who he is, what he wants, and what he will do. The evil demon Alastair in the TV show *Supernatural* used this same principle to get what he wanted. Every day Alastair put Dean on his torture chamber rack in hell and made him the same offer: To keep getting sliced and cut up or help him

Villainous Weapons of Persuasion

torture other souls. It took 30 years (in hell's time) to do it, but eventually his Relentless and Persistent Contact worked and Dean succumbed. Frankly, it's so effective, it even works *on* the bad guys — such as Jesus's parable in the Bible about the unjust judge who lacks compassion, but who is Relentlessly and Persistently Contacted by a poor widow, seeking justice. The judge stubbornly keeps rejecting her demands until, eventually, he honors her request so she finally goes away.

More:

Besides being used by demons, monsters, and world-class nags, Relentless and Persistent Contact works so consistently and reliably, it has also been…

Routinely Used By The Most Persuasive Men Who Ever Lived!

Take for example, the great Gary Bencivenga, who I mentioned earlier.

He once talked about an insurance salesman who got rich selling expensive insurance to wealthy businessmen he contacted Relentlessly and Persistently for months. In fact, he said it took an average of nine calls to finally get a hold of his leads.

And then there's 1-800-Got-Junk.

They tried for years to get on Oprah, contacting her day after day after day, with no luck. Until, eventually, they contacted one of her producers at just the right time where they needed a story idea, and they happened to be top of mind due to all the Relentless and Persistent Contact. And as a result…

They Made A Fortune!

Big broadcasters and TV shows do the same.

Think about talk radio giants like Rush Limbaugh or late-night TV kings like the late Johnny Carson (arguably the most popular man in America in his day). Their shows, their popularity, their audiences,

Villainous Weapons of Persuasion

their line of advertisers clamoring to pay them for ad time... wouldn't be nearly as big if their shows were only aired once per week instead of Relentlessly and Persistently aired every weekday.

The great Gary Halbert also used Relentless and Persistent Contact.

But, he did it in a slightly different way:

He owned a company where they would pick a popular last name, find that family name's ancient heraldic crest, and sell that crest to people with that name. But, they needed a way to translate these crests from ancient heraldic French. The only person who could do it where he lived was an alcoholic who worked at the Good Will, and it was slowing their progress. So he went to the library with the artist who re-created the crests, and found some encyclopedias that would let them translate the crests. Problem was, the encyclopedias were non-circulating. So he asked the library if he could check them out, and they said no. He asked again, and was told no. Again, he asked, and again, another no. But he kept asking over and over and over until, finally…

He Walked Out with the Books!

The artist who was with him noted:

> **"I counted, and you asked him 27 times before he said yes."**

Gary's response:

> **"I had to keep asking until I got the right answer."**

I even use this powerful principle of persuasion as an email specialist.

I utilize Relentless and Persistent Contact — via daily emails — to dominate my competition with ease — as it gives me top-of-mind positioning, creates "luck" out of thin air by always placing me in the right place at the right time (i.e., when someone is ready to buy), and, if I do it right, makes me…

Impossible to Ignore!

All of which is why, if you want to persuade someone to do something, Relentless and Persistent Contact will

Villainous Weapons of Persuasion

move mountains — and work on even the most stubbornly closed and apathetic minds.

Simple?

Yes.

Easy?

Not necessarily. Which is why doing it makes you stand out head and shoulders from the bleating herd, and exponentially increases your chances of success.

8

-

The Shameless Secret of Having Celebrity-Like Preeminence

"Apollo Creed vs. the Italian Stallion. Sounds like a damn monster movie."

— Apollo Creed
Rocky

Apollo Creed from the *Rocky* movies had all the marks of a great Villain as described in my other two books in this Villains of Influence series.

Such as his Superior Confidence... his Villain's Mask of Authority (with his multiple creative self-given titles)... his Impact via use of entertainment and showmanship.... his Obsession with being the best... his Specialization at boxing... his Patience to find the perfect opponents to maximize profits and career goals... his Mission to stay the greatest boxer in the world... his Willpower to do

Villainous Weapons of Persuasion

whatever it took to win.... his penchant for Thinking Big... his skill at creating Vision selling his idea of fighting an unknown contender to the public... his Dramatic Demonstration in how he showed up in the ring... his ability to create Curiosity to make his matches huge events... and his Relentless and Persistent Contact with the public — which he did via another Villainous Weapon of Persuasion:

Shameless Self Promotion.

Few have the Willpower to do this.

But this attribute can not only hasten the speed at which you get the things you want — celebrity status, money, power, fame, privilege denied other men, dames, and the list goes on — it can also give you the raw persuasive power of...

Preeminence!

What that means is this:

Wherever you go, whatever you do, whatever the status of the people you want to influence... preeminence means you enter the room coming from a position of them already knowing of you, already trusting you, and, most important of all, already respecting you.

This gives you priority from those you wish to persuade.

It gives you a fair hearing from even the most jaded of skeptics.

And, it counters any negative publicity about you, lies about you, or the wicked schemes of those who are envious of you. Shameless Self Promotion is also vital if you want to control the "Narrative" about you. The great advertising man Bruce Barton summed it up perfectly when he said the following to the heads of U.S. Steel, when they requested to pull their advertising from Bruce's advertising agency:

> "You are going to have national advertising whether you want it or not…It is the advertising given you by politicians with axes to grind, by newspapers that hope to build

Villainous Weapons of Persuasion

circulation by distorting your ads, by all other operators in the field of public opinion, some unfriendly and some merely misinformed."

As far as the "how to's" of self-promotion:

I refer you to any of the reputable books, trainings, and courses on the subject — including my own Shamelessly Self Promoted trainings at

www.BenSettle.com.

But for now, the most critical thing to understand and accept is…

The Importance of Being in the Business Of Being "You."

Great Villains make no apology, excuse, or denial about who and what they are — good or bad. The good is Shamelessly Promoted, and the bad is a Skeleton made to Dance.

And it goes beyond just great Villains like Apollo Creed.

It also applies to great inventors like Thomas Edison.

Or great entertainers like Frank Sinatra.

Or great actors like Steve McQueen.

Or great painters like Pablo Picasso.

Or great writers like Stan Lee.

Or great businessmen like Andrew Carnegie.

Or any of the great men who have accomplished more than 99.9% of other men will ever or have ever achieved. These men were not in the business of being an "inventor", or a "celebrity", or a "investor", or a "writer", or a "singer", or a "businessman"… no, these and other great men in history — as the esteemed Dan Kennedy teaches in his "7-Figure Academy" course — were (or still are) in…

The Self-Aggrandizement Business.

i.e., In the business of being themselves.

This is the first step for using Shameless Self-Promotion.

Villainous Weapons of Persuasion

So, get comfortable with it.

Think hard about it.

Then, implement and watch it create compliance and obedience to your commands.

Best part?

The preeminence that Shameless Self Promotion grants you is like a super power. And you can begin to possess it today, simply by making the decision to.

9
-
The Fastest Way to Get Unquestioned Compliance from People Ever Invented

"Ah, mother of God, would you look at the time? When you came here, you had an hour. Now it's less."

— Lex Luthor
Batman vs Superman: Dawn of Justice

In the movie *Batman vs Superman: Dawn of Justice*, Lex Luthor plots getting Batman and Superman to fight. And what results from his devious machinations is a Dramatic Demonstration of another powerful Villainous Weapon of Persuasion when:

> 1. Lex pushes Lois Lane off a building, knowing Superman will save her

Villainous Weapons of Persuasion

2. Lex then shows Superman various photos of his kidnapped mother Martha Kent

3. Lex tells Superman if he doesn't kill Batman his henchmen will burn Martha alive

4. Lex also gives Superman a "carrot" to persuade him to not only do the job, but do it <u>fast</u>

And that "carrot" is…

An Urgent Deadline!

Nothing gets done without a deadline.

Doesn't matter if it's something trivial, like a book report or a specific time and date to order a product to get it at a discount… or something "life or death", like a kidnapper's ransom letter demanding money by a certain time or terrorists threatening to set off bombs if they don't get what they want, when they want it.

Point is, Urgent Deadlines persuade people to take immediate action.

And they get this immediate action by creating the one thing that can bring down the most stubborn Adversary's resolve and resistance:

Neediness!

Threatening to take away a discount…

The imminent removal of a perk…

Seeing others bidding (such as in an auction) against them…

Or taking away something desirable if someone doesn't give you what you want at the appointed time…

All these Urgent Deadlines create neediness. And neediness, as detailed in *Persuasion Secrets of the World's Most Charismatic & Influential Villains*, is as deadly to a Villain as kryptonite is to Superman.

That's the bad news.

The good news?

If neediness is tamed… if it's mastered… and if it's *used* as a Villainous Weapon of Persuasion… it can…

Villainous Weapons of Persuasion

Almost Force People To Quickly Comply With Your Commands!

This is true whether it's Simon Gruber in *Diehard 3,* making John McClane endure humiliation, pain, and threat of destruction (on himself and civilians) to complete tasks at certain times… or the demon Lilith in *Supernatural,* giving Dean one year to figure a way out of his contract or be dragged down to hell… or the Hulk during the "Count Down" storyline, when he had to find a cure for a poison given to him by the Villainous Mad Man or die.

Urgent Deadlines make people take action.

And, they make people take that action…

As Fast as Humanly Possible!

All of which is why, when you want someone to comply, use an Urgent Deadline. It doesn't matter if it's to get your customers to buy from you, to get your kids to do their chores, or even to get your dame to be ready on time.

Best part:

They'll be quick about complying, too.

Imposing Urgent Deadlines has many benefits. Don't delay using them whenever you wish to persuade people to do something.

Villainous Weapons of Persuasion

10

How to "Defang" the Snakes of Slander, Smears, and Personal Attacks

"Heh. You got me."

— Walter White
AKA Heisenberg
Breaking Bad

Let's revisit the Villainous Walter White again.

One of his best moments of Villainy is when he reaches the pinnacle of his power, and his DEA agent brother-in-law Hank starts to piece together Walter's secret. Hank finds a note written by someone Walter had once worked with. The note is addressed to "W.W." And Hank, on some police intuition level, suspects W.W. could refer to "Walter White."

So, he asks, in a disarming, joking manner, if Walter is this mysterious W.W.

Walter's response?

He doesn't panic.

Doesn't get defensive.

And, doesn't even let it phase him.

Instead, he simply admits (sarcastically):

"Heh. You got me."

End of conversation.

As far as Hank is concerned, not only is Walter not W.W., but he probably even felt silly for suspecting his underachieving high school chemistry teacher brother-in-law was the king of New Mexico's meth producing underworld.

And guess what?

This is what one of the most devastating Villainous Weapons of Persuasion you can ever use looks like, known as…

"Agree and Amplify"

This means, you agree with attacks, smears, accusations, slander, or

Villainous Weapons of Persuasion

insinuations made against you… and then "amplify" them into the realm of absurdity. Do it correctly, and it instantly and automatically makes your attacker look foolish to bystanders, and sometimes even feel foolish for attacking you in the first place.

Doing so is a Dramatic Demonstration of your Supreme Confidence.

And, it quite effectively…

Defangs the "Snakes" Of Slander, Smears, And Personal Attacks!

It also steals all of your attacker's power in one quick reply.

And instead of you being on the defense explaining yourself or your actions, your attacker goes on defense, and has to explain (to you or to themselves in their own minds) why they dared try.

All of which is why, instead of fearing attacks, smears, criticism, or questions…

You Will Start to Welcome Them!

They become gifts, handed to you by your attackers. Like in certain forms of kung fu, you don't try to stop the negative energy and attacks coming at you.

You instead receive and accept them.

And then…

Use That Energy Against Your Adversary!

It's like snatching a mugger's gun from his hand and using it against him.

And so, it is with Agree and Amplify.

For example:

I once saw a man (who is a natural at Agree and Amplify) get called "stupid" by his wife, which he ignored. Then, a little later, when she asked for his help with something he didn't want to do, he simply said:

"Are you talking to Stupid?"

Villainous Weapons of Persuasion

… and made her do the task on her own.

Needless to say, she promptly apologized, and never called him stupid again.

In my own business, a once-famous rapper tried to smear some of my customers as "Nazis" and "White Supremacists" because they did not like his music and disagreed with his socialist views. Somehow, I got roped into the discussion, too, and he started trying to label me with the same names. But, while most people would run away, get defensive, or, worse, apologize (you can see this happen every day on the internet)… I Agreed and Amplified by…

Having a "Write" Supremacist Sale On One of My Products About Writing.

A sale I dedicated to the has-been rapper publicly, repeating exactly what he said so my readers knew the full context, and that nabbed my business almost $30,000 in sales in five days. All from accepting the attack, then using it to my benefit.

How about some more examples...

Let's say someone labels you as being gay to challenge your masculinity:

> **"Yep, just write out my gay confession and I'll sign it."**

Or threatens to report you to some authority:

> **"Make sure you spell my name right..."**

Or calls you a racist:

> **"Finally! A chance to wear my brand spanking new signed Hitler KKK Grand Puba robe!"**

Or asks how many women you've cheated on your woman with:

> **"You mean just today?"**

Or accuses you of have having a small penis:

> **"Maybe, but my chode is like a double wide!"**

One of the most amusing examples of Agree and Amplify is from Donald

Villainous Weapons of Persuasion

Trump. Shortly before he was elected president, he was asked about a magazine headline calling him "Hater In Chief." Most politicians would have deflected, apologized, and tried to convince the viewers they aren't really angry or mad.

Trump's response?

> **"...I do hate what's happening to America so in that way, maybe it's a very accurate depiction."**

Anyway, the message is clear:

Whenever you are attacked or accused, Agree and Amplify. Whenever your character is dragged through the mud, Agree and Amplify. Whenever you are challenged by an angry protestor, a skeptical lead, or even a bitchy dame, Agree and Amplify.

Wield this Villainous Weapon of Persuasion wisely...

And You Will Be Virtually Immune To Attacks, Smears, or Character Assassination.

All of which will give you tremendous peace of mind.

Tremendous social positioning when someone tries to personally attack you.

And, tremendous influence over those who observe you do it.

That wraps up this Villains of Influence trilogy. I hope you enjoyed these 10 powerful Villainous Weapons of Persuasion. And, even more importantly, I hope you use them, and they make you not only a better person, but a more persuasive and influential Villain, too.

For an ongoing "Villainous" education in email marketing, copywriting, selling, and persuasion, go here next:

www.BenSettle.com

Villainous Weapons of Persuasion

Dastardly Disclosures & Disclaimers

All trademarks and service marks are the properties of their respective owners. All references to these properties are made solely for editorial purposes. Except for marks actually owned by the Author or the Publisher, no commercial claims are made to their use, and neither the Author nor the Publisher is affiliated with such marks in any way.

Unless otherwise expressly noted, none of the individuals or business entities mentioned herein has endorsed the contents of this book.

Limits of Liability & Disclaimers of Warranties

Because this book is a general educational information product, it is not a substitute for professional advice on the topics discussed in it.

The materials in this book are provided "as is" and without warranties of any kind either express or implied. The Author and the Publisher disclaim all warranties, express or implied, including, but not limited to, implied warranties of merchantability and fitness for a particular purpose. The Author and the Publisher do not warrant that defects will be corrected, or that any website or any server that makes this book available is free of viruses or other harmful components. The Author does not warrant or make any representations regarding the use or the results of the use of the materials in this book in terms of their correctness, accuracy, reliability, or otherwise. Applicable law may not allow the exclusion of implied warranties, so the above exclusion may not apply to you.

Under no circumstances, including, but not limited to, negligence, shall the Author or the Publisher be liable for any special or consequential damages that result from the use of, or the inability to use this book, even if the Author, the

Villainous Weapons of Persuasion

Publisher, or an authorized representative has been advised of the possibility of such damages. Applicable law may not allow the limitation or exclusion of liability or incidental or consequential damages, so the above limitation or exclusion may not apply to you. In no event shall the Author or Publisher total liability to you for all damages, losses, and causes of action (whether in contract, tort, including but not limited to, negligence or otherwise) exceed the amount paid by you, if any, for this book.

You agree to hold the Author and the Publisher of this book, principals, agents, affiliates, and employees harmless from any and all liability for all claims for damages due to injuries, including attorney fees and costs, incurred by you or caused to third parties by you, arising out of the products, services, and activities discussed in this book, excepting only claims for gross negligence or intentional tort.

You agree that any and all claims for gross negligence or intentional tort shall be settled solely by confidential binding arbitration per the American Arbitration Association's commercial arbitration rules. All arbitration must occur in the municipality where the Author's principal place of business is located. Arbitration fees and costs shall be split equally, and you are solely responsible for your own lawyer fees.

Facts and information are believed to be accurate at the time they were placed in this book. All data provided in this book is to be used for information purposes only. The information contained within is not intended to provide specific legal, financial, tax, physical or mental health advice, or any other advice whatsoever, for any individual or company and should not be relied upon in that regard. The services described are only offered in jurisdictions where they may be legally offered. Information provided is not all-inclusive and is limited to information

Villainous Weapons of Persuasion

that is made available and such information should not be relied upon as all-inclusive or accurate.

For more information about this policy, please contact the Author at the e-mail address listed in the Copyright Notice at the front of this book.

IF YOU DO NOT AGREE WITH THESE TERMS AND EXPRESS CONDITIONS, DO NOT READ THIS BOOK. YOUR USE OF THIS BOOK, PRODUCTS, SERVICES, AND ANY PARTICIPATION IN ACTIVITIES MENTIONED IN THIS BOOK, MEAN THAT YOU ARE AGREEING TO BE LEGALLY BOUND BY THESE TERMS.

Affiliate Compensation & Material Connections Disclosure

This book may contain hyperlinks to websites and information created and maintained by other individuals and organizations. The Author and the Publisher do not control or guarantee the accuracy, completeness, relevance, or timeliness of any information or privacy policies posted on these linked websites.

You should assume that all references to products and services in this book are made because material connections exist between the Author or Publisher and the providers of the mentioned products and services ("Provider"). You should also assume that all hyperlinks within this book are affiliate links for (a) the Author, (b) the Publisher, or (c) someone else who is an affiliate for the mentioned products and services (individually and collectively, the "Affiliate").

The Affiliate recommends products and services in this book based in part on a good faith belief that the purchase of such products or services will help readers in general.

The Affiliate has this good faith belief because (a) the Affiliate has tried the product or service mentioned prior to recommending it or (b) the Affiliate has researched the reputation of the Provider

Villainous Weapons of Persuasion

and has made the decision to recommend the Provider's products or services based on the Provider's history of providing these or other products or services.

The representations made by the Affiliate about products and services reflect the Affiliate's honest opinion based upon the facts known to the Affiliate at the time this book was published.

Because there is a material connection between the Affiliate and Providers of products or services mentioned in this book, you should always assume that the Affiliate may be biased because of the Affiliate's relationship with a Provider and/or because the Affiliate has received or will receive something of value from a Provider.

Perform your own due diligence before purchasing a product or service mentioned in this book.

The type of compensation received by the Affiliate may vary. In some instances, the Affiliate may receive complimentary products (such as a review copy), services, or money from a Provider prior to mentioning the Provider's products or services in this book.

In addition, the Affiliate may receive a monetary commission or non-monetary compensation when you take action by clicking on a hyperlink in this book. This includes, but is not limited to, when you purchase a product or service from a Provider after clicking on an affiliate link in this book.

Purchase Price

Although the Publisher believes the price is fair for the value that you receive, you understand and agree that the purchase price for this book has been arbitrarily set by the Publisher. This price bears no relationship to objective standards.

Due Diligence

You are advised to do your own due diligence when it comes to making any decisions. Use caution and seek the

Villainous Weapons of Persuasion

advice of qualified professionals before acting upon the contents of this book or any other information. You shall not consider any examples, documents, or other content in this book or otherwise provided by the Author or Publisher to be the equivalent of professional advice.

The Author and the Publisher assume no responsibility for any losses or damages resulting from your use of any link, information, or opportunity contained in this book or within any other information disclosed by the Author or the Publisher in any form whatsoever.

YOU SHOULD ALWAYS CONDUCT YOUR OWN INVESTIGATION (PERFORM DUE DILIGENCE) BEFORE BUYING PRODUCTS OR SERVICES FROM ANYONE OFFLINE OR VIA THE INTERNET. THIS INCLUDES PRODUCTS AND SERVICES SOLD VIA HYPERLINKS EMBEDDED IN THIS BOOK.

www.ingramcontent.com/pod-product-compliance
Lightning Source LLC
Chambersburg PA
CBHW021847170526
45157CB00007B/2974